CLASSICAL RIFFS FOR GUITAR

by Arthur Rotfield

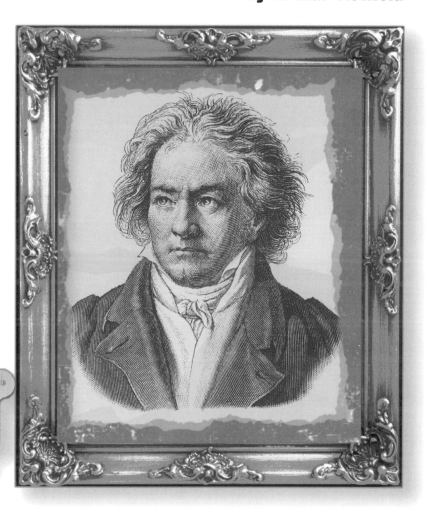

Cherry Lane Music Company
Educational Director/Project Supervisor: Susan Poliniak
Director of Publications: Mark Phillips

ISBN 1-57560-593-7

Visit our website at www.cherrylane.com

Table of Contents

——— • ———

Air on the G String (from Orchestral Suite No. 3)

Johann Sebastian Bach (1685–1750)

Bach's suites are multi-movement instrumental dance pieces in French styles, in which airs such as this one serve as a contrast. No one is certain, but Bach most likely composed this richly orchestrated work in 1731 during his Leipzig period (1729–1736). The lean, long lines of this piece sound best with another guitar playing the smooth and flowing chord progression.

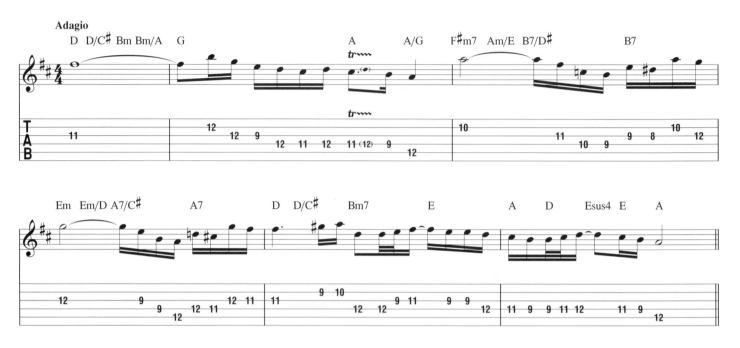

Jesu, Joy of Man's Desiring (from Cantata 147)

Johann Sebastian Bach (1685–1750)

Bach composed hundreds of religious cantatas while serving as an organist/composer in various cathedrals. These cantatas featured many types of vocal writing, including arias, duets, recitatives, and chorale harmonizations. "Jesu, Joy of Man's Desiring," though frequently arranged in two-part format for classical guitar, is presented here in single-line form as a beautiful G major study in 2nd position.

4

Symphony No. 5 in C Minor (First Movement)

Ludwig van Beethoven (1770–1827)

Beethoven inherited a legacy of symphonic composition from the masters Haydn and Mozart. In 1805 he composed his monumental Symphony No. 5 in C Minor, a representative work for its rhythmic energy and thematic development, for which many believe Beethoven to be unsurpassed. The great conductor and composer Leonard Bernstein explained that it is not Beethoven's melodic, rhythmic, or harmonic skills that made him arguably the greatest composer, but his gift of knowing exactly which note should go next. Think of this as you play the opening of the symphony shown below. Notice how Beethoven effortlessly spins out continuous variations and elaborations on the basic four-note motif.

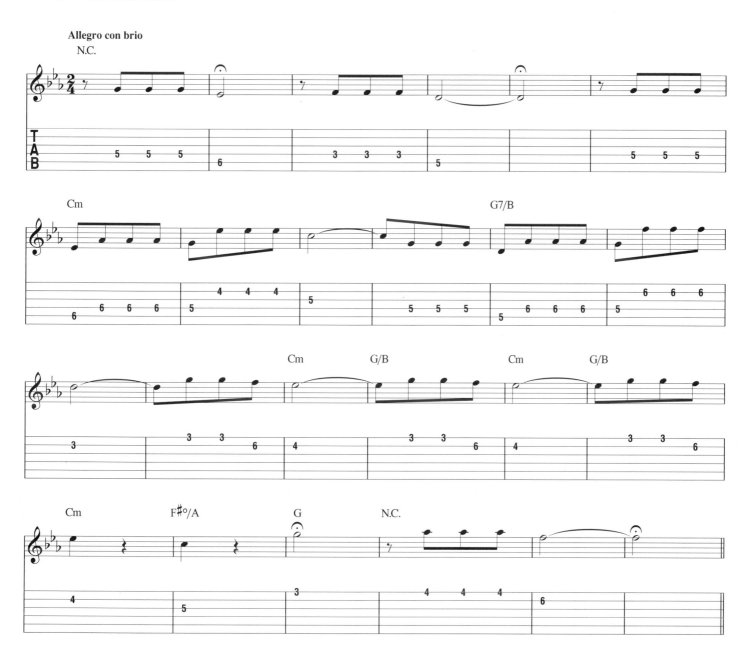

Symphony No. 9 (Fourth Movement, "Ode to Joy")

Ludwig van Beethoven (1770–1827)

———— • ————

Beethoven's final symphony was composed between 1817 and 1824. The "Ode to Joy" is the triumphant choral theme from the last movement. It is notated here in the original key of D. If you're not too much of a purist, you might want to try it with a bluegrass feel, as heard on the *Raising Arizona* soundtrack.

Habañera (from Carmen)

Georges Bizet (1838–1875)

Nietzsche said of *Carmen*, that music is wicked, refined, and fantastic. Begin this one in 7th position and then shift to 5th position with your first finger leading the way.

Minuet (from String Quintet in E Major, Op. 13, No. 5)

Luigi Boccherini (1743–1805)

Boccherini was an extremely prolific composer, but most people would be hard-pressed to think of anything of his that rivals this theme in popularity. This minuet is sure to be heard anywhere there are string players trying to establish an elegant mood. It has been (over)used extensively in film background music in everything from *Trading Places* to *Ferris Bueller's Day Off*, and even has been quoted in a Spinal Tap song. Begin this one by sliding with your ring finger from the 17th to the 15th fret of the high E string for the quick little grace note that begins the phrase. Use a similar move with your middle finger for the B-string grace note in the second full measure.

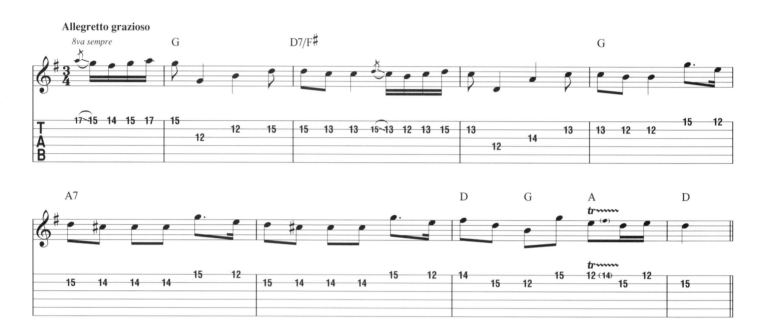

Hungarian Dance No. 5

Johannes Brahms (1833–1897)

O ne of the "three Bs" of the classical music world (along with Bach and Beethoven), Brahms ranks as one of the heirs to Beethoven and the German symphonic legacy. Here is the opening theme from one of his most famous Hungarian dances.

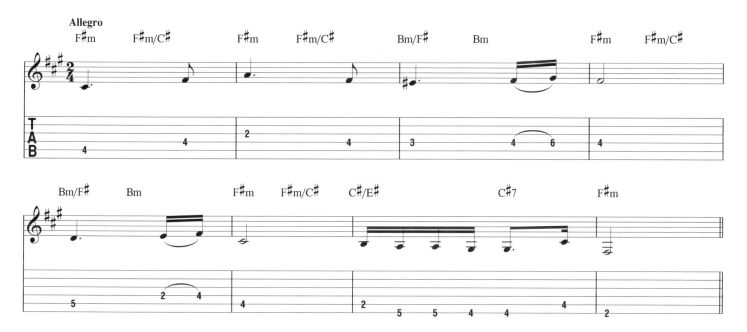

Lullaby (Wiegenlied)

Johannes Brahms (1833–1897)

——— • ———

Many people are surprised to find out that not only is this famous song in German, but it's by Brahms. It's also the perfect vehicle to see how sensitive and delicate a player you can be. The whole piece can be played in 8th position.

Marche Funebre (from Sonata No. 2 in B♭)

Frédéric Chopin (1810–1849)

————— • —————

Composer Hector Berlioz thought that the arch-romantic Chopin was "dying all his life." Hey, look who's talking! This piece is synonymous with the ominous and the macabre. There's an obviousness here that's most likely a byproduct of the March's ubiquitous appearances in countless cartoons. Try playing this as a chord/melody piece for full effect.

Prince of Denmark's March

Jeremiah Clarke (1673–1707)

————— • —————

When this stately work was wrongly attributed to Purcell, it was known as the "Trumpet Voluntary." Regal and full of pomp, this piece is widely used as a wedding processional. Here the opening theme is presented in 7th position, but don't hesitate to move to 9th position for the trills, which are easier to finger there.

Clair de Lune (from Suite Bergamasque)

Claude Debussy (1862–1918)

————— • —————

This is the melody from Debussy's beautiful "Clair de Lune." The piece is felt "in three" with triplet subdivisions (count, "1-trip-let, 2-trip-let, 3-trip-let"), except when you see "2," when you should count, "1-and, 2-and, 3-and." This Debussy classic has appeared on dozens of albums in all sorts of arrangements and was used on the *Titanic* film soundtrack.

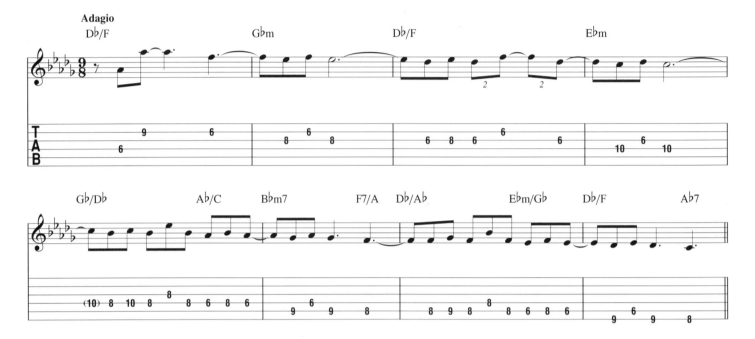

Symphony No. 9, "From the New World" (Second Movement)

Antonin Dvořák (1841–1904)

The Czech composer Dvořák composed this symphony in 1893 while serving as the director of the National Conservatory in New York. He felt American composers were not making sufficient use of their cultural heritage (i.e., the music of Native and African Americans) and decided to show them how to do so with this symphony. The fact remains that Dvořák's music is undeniably European in tradition, and nothing in this work can be labeled as truly "American." The beautiful and charming melody from the second movement is known to many as the so-called spiritual "Goin' Home," but it's not an authentic spiritual at all—it's just a song based on Dvořák's original theme.

Pavane

Gabriel Fauré (1845–1924)

•

A beautiful melody and smooth chord progression have made this *pavane* (a slow, procession-like dance) irresistible to a host of pop and jazz performers including Barbra Streisand, Bill Evans, Woody Herman, and Lee Ritenour.

Funeral March of a Marionette

Charles Gounod (1818–1893)

———— • ————

Whether you want to establish a Halloween mood or bring to mind *Alfred Hitchcock Presents,* this is your tune. And here's a really obscure reference: Roberto Benigni hums this tune repeatedly as an eccentric taxi driver in the 1991 film *Night on Earth*. Perform the quick little grace note adorning the second D with a pull-off from your pinky to your ring finger.

Morning (from Peer Gynt Suite)

Edvard Grieg (1843–1907)

———— • ————

In 1875, Edvard Grieg, a student of Schumann and Liszt, composed the incidental music for the Henrik Ibsen play *Peer Gynt* and arranged an orchestral suite of the same music for concert performance. The result is a collection of great themes of depth and character. Here is "Morning," one of many Grieg themes that has been used again and again in film and television.

In the Hall of the Mountain King (from Peer Gynt Suite)

Edvard Grieg (1843–1907)

———— • ————

Another memorable tune from the suite is this one in B minor. Consider it coincidence or concinnity, but compare the use of the 6–5 motion in the endings of this example and in "Morning."

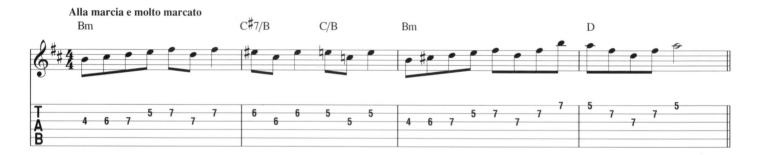

Rondeau (from Symphonic Suite No. 1)

Jean-Joseph Mouret (1682–1738)

Another work from the middle Baroque, Mouret's "Rondeau" is also a traditional wedding processional. Many will recognize this as the theme from PBS's *Masterpiece Theatre.* Play this one entirely in 9th position.

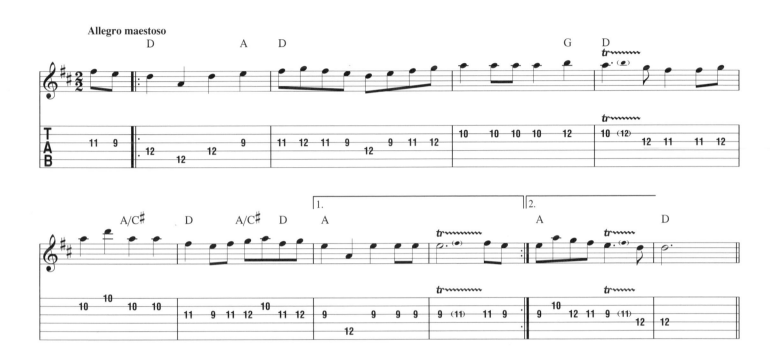

A Little Night Music (First Movement)

Wolfgang Amadeus Mozart (1756–1791)

——————— • ———————

This piece is from a *serenade*—generally a light, multi-movement work—and one of Mozart's most popular and frequently performed compositions. Here is the lively and spirited opening to the first movement. If you're striving for authenticity, note that true Baroque trills (such as those found in measures 6 and 8) begin with the *higher* of the two pitches employed.

Overture to The Marriage of Figaro

Wolfgang Amadeus Mozart (1756–1791)

One of Mozart's greatest works, this opera was composed when he was 31. The overture presents us with a frenzied eighth note passage, complete with chromatic passing and neighbor tones, to be played in 4th position. In measure 8, Mozart contrasts the narrow and winding movement of the opening bars with a grand, arpeggiated melody; move to 7th position to play this section of the theme.

Piano Concerto No. 21 in C (Second Movement)

Wolfgang Amadeus Mozart (1756–1791)

———— • ————

The Piano Concerto No. 21, composed in 1785, is from a period in which Mozart was especially prolific in writing for the keyboard. In fact, this was his eighth piano concerto in less than two years. This piece contains a beautiful and famous slow movement in F, the concerto's subdominant key, making for a C–F–C tonal scheme. The first part of the theme is presented below. Notice that one of Mozart's favorite compositional devices—the appoggiatura—appears here as strongly accented chromaticism in bars 3 and 6 where it creates a sense of longing and deep feeling. The displaced melody in bars 7–10 is considered a unique innovation. Play the C and D on the high E string with your pinky, and then follow each with index-finger pitches on the low E string. Begin the descending 16th note line in measure 10 with your middle finger.

Symphony No. 40 in G Minor (First Movement)

Wolfgang Amadeus Mozart (1756–1791)

——— • ———

Mozart's last three symphonies, of which this is the centerpiece, were composed during the summer of 1788. In addition to being one of the most exquisite symphonies in the literature, the opening is one of the most famous in all of classical music. In the original orchestration, the theme is begun by the strings, which descend quickly in measure 13 to longer, sustained tones that accompany the melody in the woodwinds.

Can-Can (from Orpheus in the Underworld)

Jacques Offenbach (1819–1880)

———— • ————

Offenbach was a child prodigy, both as a composer and a cellist. He is best remembered as the composer of great operettas, including *The Tales of Hoffman* and *Orpheus in the Underworld*. Some of you may have grown up hearing the "Can-Can" used in supermarket commercials, or maybe you know the ska version by Bad Manners. Regardless, this fast dance is always fun.

This is the first part of the theme. The positions change often here, so here's how to play it. Begin in 10th position, and then move to 12th position in bar 3 for the C (fret it with your second finger), before returning to 10th position in measure 5. Begin the final 8 measures in 15th position, with your pinky extended to catch the ultra-high B on the 19th fret. Two measures later, start the eighth note phrase with your second finger, putting you temporarily in 14th position before climbing back up to the high B.

Here is the rest of the theme, played entirely in 4th position save for the high G in the 7th measure. Simply extend your pinky here to catch it, and then slide down a fret to F♯ and continue the descending line.

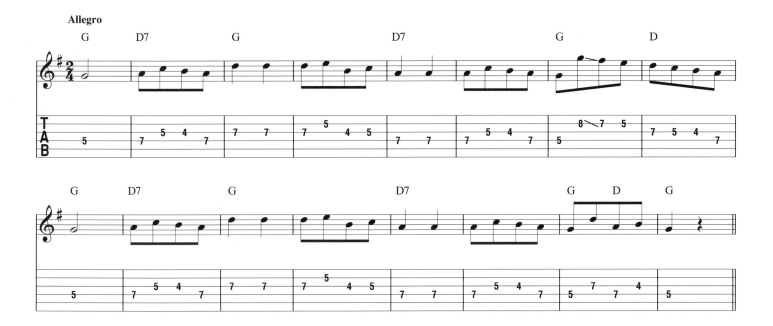

Flight of the Bumblebee (from The Tale of Tsar Saltan)

Nikolai Rimsky-Korsakov (1844–1908)

———— • ————

"The Flight of the Bumblebee" is taken from Rimsky-Korsakov's 1899 opera based on a poem by Alexander Pushkin. It was later rearranged by the great Jascha Heifetz as a violin showpiece. Countless musicians on all instruments use it as a demonstration of their virtuosity. Here's a general tip about fingering that will take you far—start each descending figure with your pinky and double up on low notes with your index finger as necessary. BZZZZ!

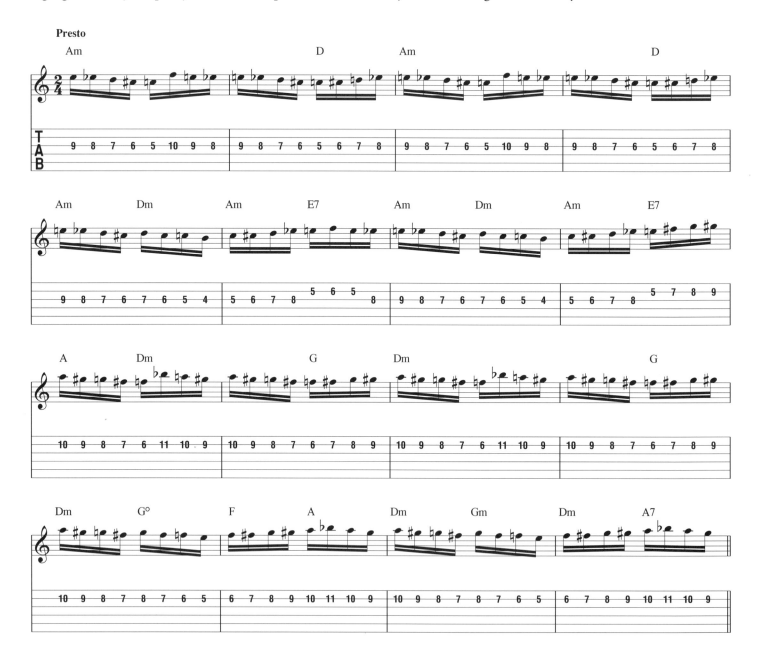

Overture to The Barber of Seville

Gioacchino Rossini (1792–1868)

———— • ————

This is the E minor theme from Rossini's 1816 operatic masterpiece *The Barber of Seville.* The trickiest parts are the pull-off figures in bars 3 and 7, all of which begin with the pinky. This one just drips with intrigue and suspense.

Overture to William Tell

Gioacchino Rossini (1792–1868)

———— • ————

Whether you know the *William Tell* overture from *The Lone Ranger, A Clockwork Orange,* or even *The Muppets Take Manhattan,* it is certainly easy to see that the piece jives with Rossini's dictum: "Delight must be the basis and aim of this art. Simple melody—clear rhythm!" Because of the brutally fast tempo, you might have trouble getting the A string to "speak" in bars 10–15 of the second example, especially if it's a light gauge string, in which case you should pick closer to the bridge for more rebound and definition.

Here is the soft opening, full of brightness and morning air.

This is the brilliant and blazing main theme.

Ave Maria

Franz Schubert (1797–1828)

Schubert said of his Ave Maria, "I never force myself into a devout mood, and never compose such hymns or prayers except when I am unconsciously inspired by Her. Then, however, it is generally real, true devotion." Accordingly, many have been won over by this moving work, and in addition to its performances by numerous operatic stars, "Ave Maria" has been recorded by pop singers as diverse as Perry Como, Mario Lanza, and Aaron Neville.

The slurs here indicate hammer-ons and pull-offs to match the melismatic character of the original. You'll find that because of these slurs, you'll need to move around the neck quite a bit, but the results are smooth, expressive, and well worth mastering. The melody is presented here in its entirety.

The Happy Farmer (from Album for the Young)

Robert Schumann (1810–1856)

———— • ————

The great 20th-century composer Igor Stravinsky greatly admired Schumann. Here is a particularly well-known and picturesque theme from Schumann's most important collection for the young.

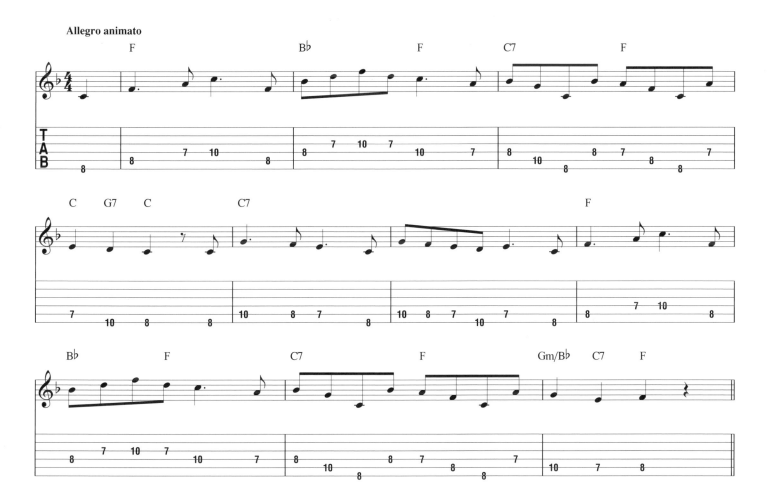

On the Beautiful Blue Danube

Johann Strauss, Jr. (1825–1899)

If Vienna has a theme song, this must be it—though, of course, it could be the theme song for space stations as well after its brilliant use in *2001: A Space Odyssey.* This gentle melody grows with a buoyant rhythm and ever-expanding melodic intervals. The design is clearly wavelike on both a small and large scale.

Waltz of the Flowers (from The Nutcracker)

Pyotr Il'yich Tchaikovsky (1840–1893)

———— • ————

Tchaikovsky composed *The Nutcracker* in 1892, late in his life. This is the famous waltz theme. Of particular interest are the ever-escalating chromatic climbs and the use of rests on the first beats of measures in the middle section for added rhythmic vitality. Remember the water ballet in *Caddyshack*? Roll over Tchaikovsky!

Skater's Waltz

Emile Waldteufel (1837–1915)

———— • ————

Waldteufel was essentially a top bandleader/composer of the late 1800s. He directed court balls in Paris and also toured Europe, conducting his own orchestral dances and waltzes. This tune has a jazz-like sound as a result of the 7ths, 9ths, and 13ths.

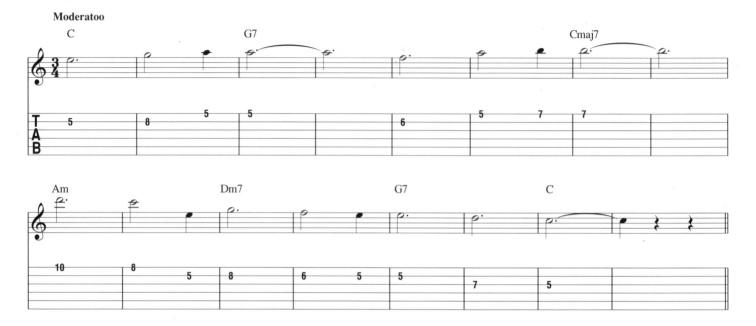